# Let the Teenage Years Begin

ABBEY WOOLGAR

Copyright © 2013 Abbey Woolgar

All rights reserved

ISBN-10: 1492939617

ISBN-13: 978-1492939610

## Dedication

How rude of me. In 'Just Another Mum' there was no mention in the dedication of the two stars that gave me so much to write about, Zac and Walt this one is for you. You give me so much and more, just keep being you, that way mum can earn more money from millions of book sales!

And in memory of the old Jasper dog (1999 – 2013) you taught us a lot.

# Contents

Fingers crossed

Goodbye old friend

Celebrate the good times

Normal is so overrated

School days, the best days of our lives

Sex, lies, videotape and a hint of music thrown in for good measure

It's really still just the beginning

*Let the Teenage Years Begin*

# Fingers crossed!

As a forty-plus year old mother, I should know that by now trying to beat my children in a spur-of-the-moment bouncing and flapping competition was bound to end in pain. On the bright side however, it has made me sit down and write the second part of Just Another Mum. The first review I got on Amazon was *"Really enjoyed this book, made me laugh out loud, so well observed. Felt like I was there. Just wish it had been longer."* So I figure there is no harm in writing more.

People have joked with me about writing the reviews and rating the first book myself. I can assure you that I could not have written these:

*"Anybody who knows Abbey will recognise the style in this book. She writes in exactly the same excited, self-effacing informative way that she talks. Once I had started reading this book I couldn't put it down till I had finished. The many anecdotes really help to bring to life the challenges and joys of bringing up autistic twins and I found the story about one of the boys confusing urinal with occupied hot tub amusing and challenging given that I was reading in the bath. I would recommend this to anybody who wants the inside track in bringing up autistic children - the challenges and some fantastic ways of overcoming them.*

*Buy it now."* Two reasons for not writing this one; 1. I had to look up the word self-effacing and 2. I don't read in the bath as the boys are usually in the vicinity firing off a round of questions, we call this their chunter time.

*"This book gives ideas for solving many problems that other mothers of children with autism must face every day. I don't have children with autism and did not really understand what autism was until I read this book. The stories in the book are easy to read, not too long, yet very informative, realistic and amusing all at once. A great read."* Reason for not writing this one; I have the mental fatigue of having children with Autism.

*"When I got my copy I thought I'd just flick through it. 20 minutes later I was still reading - laughing out loud and remembering how hard it was in the early days with the boys... Colin, Abbey, Walt and Zac - keep moving forward, I am proud to know you! You taught me a lot. Sue"* Reason for not writing this one; I am not called Sue!

Plus these comments are not at all what I would write about myself after all I am just another mum. I received an e-mail for a meeting I was due to attend. It read:

***"COFFEE MORNING THURSDAY 14th March 2013 - RSVP by Friday, 8th March***

*Dear Parent/Carer*

*We would like to invite you to attend our coffee morning on Thursday, 14th March at 11.00am. There will be a guest speaker who specialises in ASD; she also has a wealth of information regarding special educational needs. It will be a great opportunity for an informal chat and to share experiences.*

*For further information or if you have any questions please contact me at the school."*

When I arrived at the meeting I asked the lady who had organised it: "Who is the guest speaker today?"

I was promptly told, "Er, you." I was so pleased I had turned up that morning as like everyone, there are days when I think can I really be bothered! Just because I have written a book and can talk the back legs of a donkey about my children and our experiences does not make me an expert or specialist, I will always just be Zac and Walt's mum and I still think I have a long way to go to be a specialist or an expert at it.

I get quite embarrassed when someone sees me in the local shopping centre and says "Oh hello, how are you?" I have one of those faces that must instantly say "Who are you and why are you asking me how I am?" Because they always follow it up straightaway with "How are those lovely boys of yours, we do miss them" or "Please say hi to Zac and Walt for us, how are they doing?"

The best one was when we went to the local McDonalds and I queried how old young people had to be to get a part time job there. The lady instantly recognized me as Walt and Zac's mum; I had no idea who she was. Before answering my question she said, "Do you know they taught us so much when they came to the school, we were dreading having twins with Autism. I remember standing with all the other lunchtime assistants and thinking "oh this is going to be a nightmare" but do you know they were so lovely and we couldn't get enough of them" Of course I should have thanked her for her kind words, instead I simply said "So when can they start and if you could put in a good word for them that would be great." Of course writing the first book certainly didn't bring me fame or fortune but it did mean I felt like I had actually finished something.

When I explained to Zac and Walt that I had written a short story about them and that I had self-published it, they said simply, "So, does this mean you are unemployed?" "No," I replied. "There is a difference between self-employment and unemployment". I gave the usual long and rambling differences, which went right over their heads.

A few weeks later Walt sat in the bath and announced, "Mum, when I grow up I want to be just like you."

That was a proud 'mum moment' indeed, but of course it proved short-lived. "So you mean you would like to be self-employed like me?" I said, hoping that he would explain some great moneymaking idea that meant I could retire. Instead, he immediately replied, "No, I want to have just as many speeding tickets as you!"

We have been exploring work as a concept with them as soon they will need to think about their future career plans. Zac has decided that when it is time to arrange his work experience we are to write to the Queen to arrange to cut her grass. Although, having written that Zac wanted to be a planet or a vending machine in "Just Another Mum" this option seems a little easier.

Walt has decided that he would like to go and try selling cars at the local BMW/Mini garage for his two weeks of work experience. He told us there are two reasons; it is near to Tesco and that means he could go and buy a cheese and onion sandwich every day and that he would like to have a company car. His face was a picture when we told him that there were two reasons that he wouldn't be able to have a company car! He said "Well if I can't do work experience at that garage, then does this mean I can drive the cars at the car wash by Tesco then?"

*Abbey Woolgar*

# Goodbye old friend

I should start by saying that in "Just Another Mum" I described something that was totally wrong.

I wrote, "We have two dogs that Zac and Walt quite frankly find disgusting and annoying." However, it became apparent that this was so untrue when our West Highland Terrier, Jasper, decided that his time had come to say goodbye.

Between Christmas and New Year we went to visit family. In the house we left behind a snarling, growling Jasper. When we returned, some three hours later, we discovered what can only be described as a rag doll. Jasper had become limp from head to toe; something we would see a lot of over the next few weeks.

Our first thought was that Jasper had had a stroke. I said to Colin that night, "I think he may not be with us in the morning." To which Colin replied, "Let's just wait and see what happens". The next morning, I opened the door and promptly had my ankle bitten by the little rascal!

A week later, the same thing happened, a very limp and sorry for himself, Jasper. So we promptly arranged a trip to the vet. A

*Let the Teenage Years Begin*

rigorous set of tests showed that everything was okay but that a course of antibiotics would be a good idea and that if he was no better by the weekend we should take him in for a scan. The next day he was back to his normal vacuum-cleaner-attacking self.

The treatment of antibiotics finished and Jasper returned to his limp rag doll state. At this point I felt that we should explain to the boys that Jasper might well not be with us for much longer.

Zac said, "Oh well, Spencer is my dog, Jasper belongs to Walt!"

And so it began every day I would collect the boys from school whereupon Walt would ask, "How is Jasper? Have you given him his tablets?" Walt would make sure that I had done everything possible to keep the old fella going while he had been at school. As soon as we walked into the house Walt would make sure that Jasper was comfortable, that he had the right toys in his bed, that he had consumed the right amount of food and water. Jasper snarled indignantly and always looked bemused by the sudden attention.

Jasper escaped 'death row' three times but each and every time, Walt became more and more upset about Jaspers imminent departure.

Jasper had a scan followed by a biopsy

and the vet concluded that Jasper had an inoperable mass in his liver and that his body was shutting due to old age.

The following morning, Jasper's lifeless nature was put down to the sedative administered to him by the vet. By the afternoon I didn't like the look of him; there had been no vacuum chasing, no postman snarling and no growling at Spencer. I rang the vet and booked Jasper in for 4.50pm, and made a mad dash to collect the boys from school at 4.15pm. We arrived home at 4.35pm as the garage door closed onto my head I was reminded by the boys that we had to be back at school by 5.20pm for Parents Evening. Ah, the joys of being a parent and dog owner.

After throwing boys, Jasper and myself into the car, and driving so as not to gain any more points on my licence, we arrived at the vet's with three minutes to spare. I turned to them and said "nothing like the just in time principle." Walt had cried and complained about my choice of apparently 'sad' music all the way there but at the very moment I opened the door to take Jasper into to see the vet, Walt out of nowhere said, "Don't cry because it is over; smile because it has happened."

I left the boys in the car. I didn't want them to see that I would be upset if we had to say goodbye to the old man. When the

*Let the Teenage Years Begin*

vet said, "Let's try some steroids" all I could think was thank goodness I don't have to go and tell Walt that we have had to say goodbye. When I went back to the car with Jasper, Walt's face was something I will never forget; he beamed and said, "We'll be able to go to Parent's evening now."

A week later, Jasper really went down hill. His biopsy results had come back as 'inconclusive' and there was nothing else that could be done for him and we had to say goodbye.

Spencer reacted terribly to the loss of Jasper, and after 24 hours Walt began to ask, "When are we getting a new dog?" So, after a week of some pestering and Spencer going into what seemed like the first stages of canine depression, along came Percy, an Italian Spinone. Yes, it happened quickly, but we were not replacing Jasper, merely preserving our status as a two-dog family!

Of course, Percy still smells like a dog. This is most disagreeable to Walt, particularly when Percy has eaten his own poo or his fish dinner. I did have to have words when Walt announced, "Mum, you are starting to smell as badly as Percy" but Zac now says 'Why does Walt smell like Percy and he should really wash his hands after he has touched him" nothing like a nice bit of brotherly love.

Walt lovingly refers to Percy as 'Mop' and

15

tells him all his troubles and when I ask him to do something and then ask him why he hasn't done it he will reply, "Mop is such a distraction." Every day Walt will ask, "How has Percy's day been?" I am still hoping that one day he may say "How has your day been with Percy mum?" But I think I will have a long wait. This is a legacy for which we have Jasper to thank. To be honest, we are probably starting one of those media portrayals where dogs unlock the world of a child with Autism. Argh.

The only problem is that Zac has now started to ask, "When Spencer dies, which puppy shall we get? And what shall we call him?" Let's just hope Zac and Walt do not think people are replaceable like dogs.

Having a puppy in the house again has reminded me that dogs really are on the spectrum, we would always describe Jasper as a dog with ASD; he always followed the same route, he liked his own space and was a bit snarly and grumpy when you didn't understand what he wanted but having a puppy revealed even more Autistic traits like; running around in circles, chasing things that catch their attention, doing disgusting things, and being anxious about new places. But, of course, my favourite is: they understand only simple commands!

Having a new puppy and children on the spectrum has bought many new challenges.

One stressful Monday morning, I had gone upstairs to get ready to walk the boys to school at 7.50am. I was in the bathroom, completely naked. The doorbell rang.

For months we had been trying to explain to the boys that if the doorbell or the telephone rang, they can answer it if mum and dad are in the house.

The power of writing this instruction down for them had been totally forgotten, so instead we had resorted to yelling, "Boys answer the door, please!" Percy's arrival had not been factored into this.

On that particular morning, Zac was in one of his little foggy Monday morning trances. When Zac is in this state, he is unable to process simple sentences or commands. That particular morning proved to be a case in point.

I yelled from the bathroom, "Zac, DON'T open the door!" The emphasis was on the word don't.

Yep, you guessed it. Zac promptly opened the door and out ran Percy the puppy. I stood for a couple of seconds and thought of all the horrible things that could happen to Percy. I promptly decided that if Lady Godiva could do it riding through Coventry, there was no reason why I should not run through the streets of our neighbourhood, chasing a 13-week old puppy.

I will not forget the shock and horror on Zac and Walt's faces, particularly as one of the local boys and his sister were our callers and they were waiting to walk to school with us. Of course, Percy being a puppy stopped immediately to be fussed by them. How I was chastised for embarrassing the boys and not trusting them to have it all under control. And the school friends? Well they haven't called round since and often find it difficult to look at me if we bump into them. I chalk this up as one of those nasty embarrassing parent things that happen when you are a teenager just for my own sanity!

When this is mentioned I always gently remind Zac that he exposed himself at Crufts in front of the BBC; and therefore, I still have some way to go to be up there with him in the embarrassment stakes! That retort goes right over his head but it always makes me feel slightly better.

To make sure such an event never happens again we now have a social story™[1] affixed firmly to the front door. This reads:

### Opening the Front Door

*I open the front door ONLY if Percy and Spencer are in the kitchen or the lounge with*

---

[1] *Social Stories™ were developed by Carol Gray. A Social Story™ describes a situation, skill, or concept in terms of relevant social cues, perspectives, and common responses in a specifically defined style and format. The goal of a Social Story™ is to share accurate social information in a patient and reassuring manner that is easily understood by its audience. Although the goal of a Story™ should never be to change the individual's behaviour, that individual's improved understanding of events and expectations may lead to more effective responses.*

*the door shut.*

*I open the front door ONLY if mum and dad are in the house with me.*

*I open the front door ONLY if I know who it is.*

*I can tell the person on the other side of the door to "please wait" while I find mum or dad to help me.*

What I failed to do though was make Walt aware of this and keep up with the routine checking that the story was understood.

Back in April, just before the boys birthday, I was in the back garden mowing the lawn. Walt took it upon himself to answer the door, completely ignoring the social story™. Walt ran out to the garden to tell me that there was a big box, for his birthday, on the kitchen table. When I said "Sorry, what do you mean there is a big box on the table for your birthday?" He said, "Well, a man came and he did give me the box and I said thank you." I'll give him one thing at least he had been taken in our constant nagging about "manners maketh man" but the panic then set in.

I asked "And where is Percy?" His reply was "Its okay mum the man grabbed him." That was supposed to make me feel better. At this point I decided I should hastily go to the kitchen to see where Percy was and what was in the box. Having found Percy safely chewing on something he shouldn't have been, I opened the box and in it were 12 bottles of wine, clearly not for Walt's birthday. So I asked Walt "What did the man look like?" as there were no real obvious clues as to who had left such a lovely gift!

My immediate thoughts were that a delivery driver had got the wrong house and the poor bloke had forgotten to give Walt any paperwork because of the bolting puppy and the over excitable soon to be teenager. Walt said "The man was Steve (our neighbour) so I opened the door."

Now, I knew it couldn't have been Steve, as he was in America on business and we had been looking after his house. So I said "It can't have been Steve, he is away". Walt said "But he had glasses like Steve". So the statement "I open the front door ONLY if I know who it is" would have to be revisited. When I finally managed to piece everything together to see who the wine was from, I certainly needed a glass or two!

The new fascination and interest in the dogs has made me encourage the boys to help out with some of the basic dog ownership tasks. One fine and sunny morning, but ten minutes before we needed to leave for school, I was hurriedly hanging out washing. Zac came out to the garden and said, "Look a poo." So I asked Zac to go into the kitchen and please get me a bag. As a parent I often forget the need to be very specific. Usually if I ask Zac to get me a bag he will default to what he knows as a bag, my handbag. I have had to say on numerous occasions "no Zac I can't clear the poo up with my handbag".

On this particular morning though Zac bought me the right bag and I was chuffed to pieces and thought finally, we have cracked that poo goes in a poo bag. Zac said helpfully, "I'll pick it up." Now I should have thought, ten minutes before school, poo, school uniform and Zac don't mix but I said, "OK, I'll help you get the bag ready and then you can do it." So, I assisted him to put the bag on his hand, showed him the motion for picking it up 'dab, not grab' and then left him to it. He was very pleased with himself when he managed to bag the poo and tie the handles up. Then followed the simplest instruction, "Zac, please can you put it in the bin now, thanks."

After a few moments I thought that's a bit odd I didn't hear the bin lid, he would have walked right passed the dustbin. So I shouted "Zac where is the poo?" He replied, "It's on the kitchen table."

Yes, there it was sitting on the kitchen table (thankfully still in the bag) and so I calmly said, "Why is the poo on the table?" Bless him, he said, "I am very proud and I am going to show Walt and then put it in the bin." When I asked him which bin he pointed to the one in the kitchen. We had a bit of a chat about poo and hygiene on the way to school and I think I must have repeated, "Now I am going to have to bleach the table" about ten times. I am still learning that I need to be specific about most things even if they seem obvious to me.

*Let the Teenage Years Begin*

# Celebrate the good times

Coping with Christmas, birthdays, weddings and other formal occasions are things that parents of newly diagnosed children with ASD ask me about at my presentations. They can be ultra stressful because we all have expectations about how these events should be celebrated, but when you have a child with ASD you really have to park them elsewhere or face a stressful or disappointing day. Sometimes you have to look for the small things that have delighted your child rather than expecting them to delight in the full day. An example of this was when my in-laws treated us to a day at Santa Pod Raceway. We thought the boys would love it, the speed, the range of cars and the anticipation of who would win.

My father-in-law had got us some great grandstand seats and we had prepared the boys for the noise with ear defenders and earplugs. We took our seats and the races started. Zac couldn't cope with any of it. He screamed and cried and so I took him outside of the arena. At first you think, what a waste of time and money and you get really quite angry about missing out on an event that you wanted to enjoy with them. On this day though Zac taught me that he could enjoy something in a different way.

As we had gone into take our seats Zac had obviously clocked something he might like to have a go at. As I walked him out, with a face like thunder, he pulled me towards one of the sideshow attractions. He has always had a fascination with fish and he had spotted the fish that eat the dead skin on your feet and hands. At first I thought he just wanted to watch the fish but after about ten minutes of bouncing and flapping he indicated that he would like to actually put his hands in with the fish. After about thirty seconds of fish eating his hands, Zac was so relaxed; he was almost in some sort of fishy heavenly trance. To see him like this opened my eyes to the theory that although we expect to all experience the same thing, sometimes we need to just think about the little things that could make our lives so much easier.

I recently received this message from a parent who said her son hated Christmas and it was always a stressful event in her house:

**Subject:** *Thank you for your advice re Christmas*

**Sent:** *Wednesday, 9 January 2013 14:39*

*Hi Abbey*

*I just wanted to thank you for giving the advice of not wrapping up Edward's*

*Christmas presents, as it made a huge difference to him on the day. He is already asking for his birthday presents not to be wrapped up this year.*

*The holidays were hard with Edward being like the Duracell bunny for 2 weeks and on the go for up to 18 hours a day, but we got through it.*

*Hope you had a lovely Christmas.*

*Best wishes for the New Year.*

*Thanks.*

*Joanne*

And it's lovely when you hear that a suggestion is still working:

**Subject:** Hello

**Sent:** Saturday, 13 July 2013 15:50

*Hi Abbey*

*I don't know if you remember me from a course you spoke at last year with Lesley Harrison with your experiences on being a mum to twins with autism. The Christmas present suggestion you gave us has been a lifeline for our youngest son and he's just celebrated his birthday and once again at his request, his presents were not wrapped and it's the first time he's really enjoyed his presents on the day he received them. It's such a transformation.*

*Kind regards.*

*Joanne*

Presents can be a major issue. This year, Walt wanted a garden swing for his birthday. In "Just Another Mum" I wrote;

*"The Google search engine is usually my friend but there are some things you just cannot find. For example, the Internet is not somewhere you want to go to and type in "Penis out of zip – Image."*

I sat beside Walt and we Googled 'Adult swing' as he thought we would be able to obtain one from 'Toys R Us' or 'Early Learning'. In this case though, I had not heeded my own advice; the images of an adult swing that came up on the laptop proved most amusing and especially fascinating to a pubescent boy. I, of course, quickly informed him that this was not the type of swing we would be buying for the garden.

When they were young, each and every present could easily be a new Thomas train. A Thomas train would make their eyes light up, but present them with anything else and they would instantly throw it on the floor or say, "No thank you, not for me" This is fine until the person giving them the present is expecting the moment of delight and excitement but is actually faced with what can only be described as a 'spoilt brat'. There is only so much explaining you can do and so now we go for the easy option which, is do the present opening alone and then prepare and prime the thank you response.

Over the years Thomas has turned into Disney Pixar Cars and every year Walt is delighted when he receives a new one for his collection. He still enjoys lining them up and seeing which one he can have for next. But now that the boys are getting older it is more and more difficult to think of things that other people can buy for them and like most children they seem to have everything they need and some. For the boys most recent birthday we had decided that it would be just the four of us for present opening, thank goodness. The boys took a look at the small pile of presents and announced "Is that all" and then tore open the various cards, only to then blurt out "£10 is that all, things cost at least £20!" And when they got to the WHSmith voucher they said, "WHSmith what kind of a shop is that!" And again you might think, "ungrateful little blighters" but we know now that this is just one of the joys of ASD which is not going away even with the various chats and primed thanks. Zac and Walt just have to say what is on their minds and when you think about it you have probably received a present from someone and thought "Why the

Dickens have they got me that?" but just never said it out loud!

Presents don't always get enjoyed straightaway, they have to be given a settling in period before they are operated or appreciated. Several years ago Zac asked for a unicycle for Christmas. By the summer it finally enjoyed its maiden voyage having been sat and admired on its stand in his bedroom for eight months!

The boys are also influenced by what their peers are talking about. One Christmas, both boys had asked us for a Nerf machine gun. The one they wanted was obscene it fired foam bullets at a great rate of knots. It was the sort of thing we had never imagined that they would ask for. On Christmas morning, they were both delighted when they opened the wrapping to find the biggest piece of yellow plastic we had ever seen. It then took us an age to remove it from its packaging only to discover that each one needed eight 'D' type batteries. Something the present giver had forgotten to check.

After the ensuing tantrum we tried to explain to the boys they would have to wait until we could buy some batteries, probably on Boxing Day, every parents nightmare and that they had so many other things to enjoy. Of course this didn't go in, Zac cried for hours. After some searching – we found the local Budgens (or "Buttchins" as the boys

*Let the Teenage Years Begin*

pronounce it) was open – and some £20 later the tantrum dissipated, surprise, surprise. The guns were played with twice, when their friends came round but now they gather dust at the bottom of their wardrobes, probably with totally flat batteries!

Zac makes sure he sheds tears every Christmas day. It can be over something he has received as a present, or over something quite trivial and bizarre. Christmas just isn't Christmas in the Woolgar household unless Zac cries.

Christmas 2012 proved to be no exception, even though we thought we had cracked it. We proceeded to involve Zac in all aspects of the big build up to the day, hoping that this would alleviate his stresses and any anxiety.

Together we put up the Christmas trees. We have to have two, one for the kitchen and one in the lounge, the presents for other people <u>must</u> only go under the kitchen tree, they are not allowed to go anywhere near the family presents, how that started I will never know! We also had to let him into the secrets of what presents we had for Walt and we guaranteed he would receive all the presents he had asked for. Zac finds it very difficult to select presents that he might like, so we can usually make sure that what he does write down, he can get. We do monitor this just in case. One year he asked for a live Shark so we said that he might like to remove this, as

29

he would be disappointed.

The day passed fairly smoothly, with the exceptions of one dog being violently sick and the other peeing all over the kitchen floor but this was all taken care of by me with the aid of a couple of pear ciders. In the evening, the boys scurried up to their rooms to look at all the presents they had unwrapped.

Colin and I had just started to relax, and I recall saying to him "I think we have cracked it, no tears from Zac this year." I should have then touched some wood but in true Mr. Benn style "as if by magic..." Zac appeared at the door, tears streaming down his face. When we asked him what was wrong he simply said "School."

We are not sure how 'school' and Christmas had become mixed together in his head; it wasn't like we had given him some GCSE textbooks or stationery, god forbid! We concluded that, sometimes, it is impossible to plan for every eventuality. More pear cider was applied and we tackled the issue of 'school' late into Christmas night.

One of the most unusual aspects of celebrations with Zac and Walt is that it is never necessary to hide their gifts, unlike most parents we don't seem to have to come up with cunning ways to keep them from finding what we have bought for them. They just don't ever seem curious, they don't even try and peek through the paper.

*Let the Teenage Years Begin*

When I was about seven or eight years old, I remember one Christmas Eve being so curious as to what was hidden in my mum and dad's wardrobe that I ruined the ritual of Santa. I found the presents that Santa then subsequently left for me the following morning. I am still not sure if this was simply a ruse by my parents to save money on buying so much but I think I managed to pull off the illusion that Santa existed for another couple of years. So far, we have managed to preserve the illusion of Santa and his reindeer paying us a visit each year. We can still use the classic phrase: "Be good as Santa is watching you!" from about November. Occasionally, we receive the reply: "Does he actually exist?" to which we answer, "Of course, the spirit of Christmas is real!" Not a lie. I do wonder for how many more years we will have to make sleigh bell noises late into the night, eat mince pies, bite into raw carrots and hang up the magic door key. For now though, it's great fun, a family tradition but we just don't tell other teenagers.

Another fabled character, the tooth fairy illusion lasted only for a couple of teeth in the Woolgar house. When you have a child with ASD who experiences difficulty in sleeping, the last thing you want to do is sneak into their room and surreptitiously place a coin under their pillow. One wrong move and you're guaranteed a sleepness

31

night. Zac pretty much told us after the first tooth that she didn't exist because she had forgotten to leave £1. Our quickness to deposit the money had meant that we had only just managed to get it on the edge of the bed and by the morning it had slipped onto the floor. Clearly to Zac this meant that she had not been as he had been informed that the £1 would be under the pillow not under the bed. I think that he announced, "Well the one they have sent here is pretty rubbish at her job!"

The singing of "Happy Birthday" is not allowed in public and there is absolutely no telling others that it is a birthday celebration. When a birthday falls on a school day the stress is far too much to bear, so we usually arrange an unexplained stomach bug. This is so that I can keep my own sanity and keep the day as happy as possible and hey who hasn't pulled a sick day once in a while.

Surprisingly, Easter causes no problems at all and we have never introduced the Easter Bunny. The copious amount of chocolate consumed for breakfast is enough to get us through the day. I am not sure exactly what the boys think of Easter. Last Easter Zac queried, "When did Jesus eat the chocolate?" The difficulty is you can't just make up a spur of the moment answer because it will be remembered and repeated with "Mum you said . . ." Wikipedia is usually my source for checking these type of pressing questions although I could find nothing on Jesus eating chocolate!

It's not just the boys who get confused. My good friend, Gillian and I visited a garden centre in September to find an array of Christmas cards. One card depicted Noah on his ark dressed as Santa with all the animals frolicking in the snow. Religion is not something I know much about but I am convinced Noah is Old Testament and the birth of Christ was New Testament. My only response to the boys questions on this if they saw it would be "It's just all got very commercial" and then bang goes the magic of Christmas, probably for the rest of the boys lives. So it is probably safer just to stay away from places with the wrong visual clues.

Mother's Day, like Valentine's Day is not a big day in the Woolgar house. The phrase "It's just a way of card shops making money" is often bandied about in the run up to them. So this year I decided that I would treat myself for Mothers Day. I ordered my own card and bought my own chocolates: two big bags of peanut M&Ms. According to my theory, one bag would be from Zac and the other from Walt. After collecting the boys from school I asked them to take the card and chocolate and hide them ready for Sunday. Easy.

No. Not in the world of Zac and Walt. At

*Abbey Woolgar*

2am I woke up. This is one of the joys of being a lady of a certain age. As I turned my pillows over there 'hidden' away were my Mother's Day card and peanut M&Ms! Apparently, I would "never have found them there until Sunday" had I "not have been so old and sweaty!" I did try to argue that I was more like a Princess from the Hans Christian Andersen story 'The Princess and the Pea', but of course this went straight over their heads. Thankfully M&M's are coated so the present was saved!

*Let the Teenage Years Begin*

# Normal is so overrated

I am always asked about things like; haircuts, trips to the dentist, doctors, clothing and a whole of host of other things that people without a touch of ASD in their lives can often do without careful planning and thought.

Let me start with haircuts. When Zac and Walt were little we would put them in their highchairs, strap them down, turn up the TV and Colin would get the clippers out and give them a grade 2 all over so that the torture didn't need to happen again for at least two months. To say the boys disliked haircuts is an understatement. Sometimes we would do just half a head, have a few hours off and then try again the next day. Of course this meant that you couldn't go out and see anyone for fear that they would report us to the fashion police for crimes against Friar Tuck.

Our old neighbour, George, who in 'Just Another Mum' was mentioned for his concerns about us murdering Zac and Walt when we were washing their hair, suggested that we try his hairdresser. We had tried going to a hairdresser before, we had carefully selected a salon and a time of day that would be quiet. Then came the hairdresser a pretty blonde (The boys

35

preference) was chosen and then it began. After two minutes I was sweating, the hairdresser had cut her own finger rather than cutting off the ear of a flailing Zac and after what could only be described as a rather long ten minutes and only a few strands of hair coiffured she said, "I'm sorry but this is impossible, can I suggest that you don't bring him again." So I promptly scooped them both up and left. So we gave George's suggestion of Elaine a go.

I can now only describe Elaine as a hairstyling goddess. When she arrived for the first haircut, I decided to give her what I thought would be a challenge, so I suggested an American style bowl haircut, long on the top and blended in around the sides and the back. The tricky bit is the getting the longest length cut in a straight line.

The gauntlet was thrown down and after a relaxed hour or so both boys looked just as I had pictured. I still to this day, do not know how Elaine does it, but each and every time the boys go and see her for a haircut she gets it just right. Now they like to pick the style they want from the Internet the night before we go and take a picture along for Elaine and she works hairdressing miracles. We have told her she is never to retire. Sometimes the boys will ask her to do some strange things, one day Zac announced that he would like her to "cut all the mouldy bits off." Zac's Trichotillomania has meant that sometimes he has to have a great comb over but as long as he believes Elaine has left his hair long he is okay about the whole process.

They still wriggle and fidget when she cuts their hair and we still have to warn them that a haircut is imminent and make a planned list of who is going to sit in the chair, first, second and third but Elaine still manages to amaze us. Walt always announces that he is handsome after he has been to Elaine's and that is all you can ask.

Hair seems to be important to the boys. My hair is always a topic of discussion for them. As a lady in her forties grey hair and wrinkles are inevitable so regular trips to the hairdressers to change the colour and style are required. My hair reached the length of being able to put it up into a ponytail and the comment received from the charming Zac was simply, "Ponytails make you grumpier don't wear it like that again" So the ponytail was cut off.

Taking Zac's advice I decided to go really short, as the hairdresser cut my hair off I said. "I bet my children will say I look like a boy!" Imagine my horror when Walt saw the hairdresser's handiwork after school and announced, "Mum you look like a l-e-s-b-i-a-n!" There followed a long chat about the inappropriateness of making such a comment and how we cannot stereotype people just because of how they look. Let's hope that this has sunk in.

When I returned to the hairdressers some six weeks later she cut it shorter again. This time when I approached them they both said, "Oh no, now everyone is going to think we look like you." The most embarrassing time for Walt though came when he accompanied me to the hairdressers and we had to pop into a shop to buy a greeting card. As we entered a 'helpful' shop assistant approached us and said, "Hello, can I help you boys." This is not something any teenager wants to hear when they are out with their mum. Albeit very flattering in some way for me to be mistaken for a teenager was pretty good but the boy bit, hmmm?

Shoe shopping was a similar experience to haircuts. When they were younger Zac and Walt hated taking their current shoes off and trying on new ones. They would get very distressed in the shop and the only way we could get them to calm down would be to distract them by making lines of shoes. Now in my mind this doesn't hurt anyone, yes it may mess up a display a bit but we would always put them back.

We always choose to go to the local shopping centre late on a Friday night, when it is quiet, the theory is that we should be able to go in, get what we need and then leave quickly with a couple of bribes, or should I say rewards along the way. So one

*Let the Teenage Years Begin*

Friday evening we walked into a local well known shoe shop and started to distract the boys. In fact we were quite pleased because the boys seemed to be doing a good job of lining the shoes up on their own. The shop was very quiet in fact the staff were simply chatting amongst themselves. I think I made a couple of "uh hum" noises to see if I could draw some attention to our need to purchase some shoes. Eventually a stern lady approached us and said, "Sorry but your children have created a lot of work for us and I think you should leave." I seem to recall just standing looking at her blankly for a moment and then feeling Colin tug at my arm, indicating that we should make an exit.

We picked the boys up and left the shop. As we exited into the shopping centre walkway I said to Colin, "Did she just say that?" Before he could say "yes" I had walked right back into the shop, confronted the shop assistant and her colleagues and said "I will never shop in a your store again, you are rude and you obviously don't get children who are a little bit different. My children have Autism and that's hard enough but to have to be confronted by ignorant people like you makes it so much worse." I didn't wait to see what response they would give. We simply voted with our feet and we never went back to that outlet again.

The phrase when one door closes another one opens though was so true in this case.

We walked through the shopping centre trying to work out how we would get the boy's feet measured. Finally we decided to give another shop ago. We walked into Charles Clinkard and were greeted enthusiastically by a lovely lady called Vanessa. Vanessa has been very patient and over the years she has put up with them running out of the shop to fully test the new shoes out and just laughing when they set off the security alarms. She has had to retrieve them from underneath the seats and she has developed her pain threshold when they accidentally tread on her hand or kick her. The local John Lewis has developed a system for working with customers that are autistic but we have stuck firmly to Charles Clinkard just because they were there to pick us up from the horrors of our shopping experience at the well known shoe shop.

A few years ago that particular branch of the well known shoe shop closed down, were we surprised? I very much doubt they knew how to cope with even the most perfect child.

There are days when I feel that I have perfect children. Autism can have a whole host of advantages especially when things are written down or scheduled.

One way of achieving almost perfect children has been through setting our house rules. We sit together as a family and come up with a couple of rules each along with the consequences if one is broken. The rules are then signed and stuck up onto the notice board. The current rules are:

We should not shout at each other, we should talk (exceptions to this rule are: when someone is in danger, calling down for meals and chores!)

We should have a family TV/film night at least once a week

We must chew our food at least 10 times before swallowing!

We should think about other people in the house and the impact our actions have on them

We must remove our shoes before entering the house

On a school day we get up on time and come down to breakfast when we are asked

There will be no swearing

We should always answer when we are asked a question rather than having to repeat ourselves over and over again

We need to say "hello" and talk to people that we know

We should have regular planned tickle fights

We must not answer back (back chat) when someone tells us we need to improve our behaviour

We should relax and have fun with plenty of cuddles

We should try not to interrupt each other

We should keep the house clean and tidy and help each other to do this

The undersigned agree to theses rules. Should any of the rules be broken the consequences are listed below:

*Let the Teenage Years Begin*

| Rule Broken | Consequence |
|---|---|
| All of the above rules except: | An extra chore of mums choosing |
| Swearing | £1 will be placed the swear jar |

I should point out that the swear jar gains most of its income from me and that I have a very clean house from a lot of extra chores! The set before this included the rule that we should not fart when someone else was in the room with us except when we were in the bathroom but we all found this one far too difficult to stick to.

The other key to almost perfect children is through scheduling household chores. At the same time as the rule setting we sit and review the house chore list. Now most non-autistic children might say, "So how much money are you going to give me to do these things?" Zac and Walt still haven't grasped the concept of money and there have been days when they have been given a £10 note and then simply left it lying around, not realising what it could be used for. We are lucky though that we don't hear the immortal words "Do I have to do these chores?" Zac and Walt simply look at the schedule and get on with them. Sometimes they even trade chores with each other. The only explaining we had to do was that it would be good for them, especially when they become adults.

Each day they have two chores each to do from the list of hoovering, cooking tea on a Saturday (with help), feeding the dogs, emptying the bins, cleaning the school shoes, making the lunches for the next day, mopping the floors and putting the washing in the machine.  We hope that by mastering these things they will make great husband material.  The arranged marriage may still have to be an option but at least I will be able to sell them as 'fully house trained' and I know that if I am not there to support them that they will have a fighting chance of being independent.

We are still working on going to the shops.  The local 'Buttchins' is a very safe five-minute walk from our house.  To begin with we sent the boys together with just one or two items to buy, this did not include the bribe item, which would be their opportunity to buy something of their own choosing, usually a 'nice drink'.

We soon realised that this was a very expensive way of buying a pint of milk and we heard from a friend that they had been seen helping each other get into the fridge to reach the milk on the top shelf, rather than asking for help.  So we changed tack and started to send them alone.  Now we get arguments on whose turn it is to go.

Most teenagers would be delighted to

*Let the Teenage Years Begin*

get out of the house and go to the local shop especially with the chance to spend the loose change, but not Zac and Walt. They are afraid of the 'teenagers in skinny jeans' who are perceived to be hanging around outside. The fear of seeing someone they may know is absolutely terrifying to them. We are not sure whether they have this phobia because they don't know the latest hand slapping code used amongst their peers, or it is because they don't know what the latest street etiquette is for saying 'hello' but what we are faced with are two very introverted boys who want to hide in their clothing and hold onto us for dear life.

Because of this instinct to hide at a moments notice like a tortoise, the boys prefer to wear clothes with hoods. Yes, that makes them teenage hoodies but you can not only hide in the hood but if you are Zac you can sniff it all at the same time making you feel very safe and secure.

Recently clothing has become an issue, like most teenagers the boys are growing at a great rate of knots. They are at that stage when you buy a pair of trousers, a week later you think 'did I read the washing care instructions incorrectly or have they grown again?' Now this isn't a problem when you can find trousers that are within budget, aren't made of a material that you know won't irritate them and in the right size. We also have the added benefit of needing to find trousers that don't have flies. As I mentioned in 'Just Another Mum' we learnt very quickly that we should not use the word 'flies' to describe doing their trousers up so we have favoured the elasticated waistband. The elasticated waistband is not the best look for a teenage boy but they do prevent embarrassment when you have been to the toilet or been in your room alone and you are called downstairs. People who play sport appreciate the elasticated waistband so at the weekends the wearing of shorts or tracksuit bottoms has become acceptable.

It is said, that the London 2012 Olympics inspired most of us. Zac and Walt were no exception to this. We watched a lot of the events on the TV but we were also lucky enough to go to the Para Olympics to watch the athletics. However, the sport that caught their eye was hockey. I did not discourage watching this at all because at school this had been my favourite sport and in my early twenties and through to my early thirties I picked up my stick and played for a couple of local Norfolk women's teams. So I actively encouraged the boys to have a go.

I should explain that we had tried a whole number of sports with the boys including gymnastics, football, skiing, and golf:

Gymnastics was great and they both loved going along to a special needs group on a Saturday evening but after a while they became bored of doing the same thing. The gymnastics coach suggested that they give the mainstream sessions a go to keep their interest. We took Zac along but he absolutely hated it and said he never wanted to go back. We applied the ten times rule (try something ten times then give up for a while then try again) but he really didn't want to do it anymore.

We tried a special needs football club. Colin and I spent a fair few hours standing on a cold, wet but floodlit pitch encouraging them to join in but after watching them spinning round, looking at the sky, chewing the bibs and really generally not understanding how to play the game we decided that enough was enough and perhaps football DNA just wasn't there. We blame ourselves for this of course because neither Colin nor I support any team and we certainly don't watch it on TV or follow a particular team.

Skiing is an ongoing sport for the boys. However, recently we have watched the individual competitiveness between the boys and have decided to give this a rest for a while. Zac started to get very frustrated because he could see Walt getting higher up the slope and he would throw himself onto the snow have a tantrum and then keep hitting his legs when they wouldn't do what he expected them to. Plus, we got fed up of being branded as 'middle class' by certain professionals when they would ask what activities we took the boys to.

Zac loves nothing more than whacking golf balls and every now and again we take him up to the local driving range and play a round of crazy golf. So hockey was not dissimilar.

We have found that the boys have really taken to playing hockey. There are many reasons but I can highly recommend hockey to any parent of a child with autism for a number of reasons:

> They can merrily chew on a gum shield, you keep Sport Direct in business as you need at least one a week

> They hold a stick which curbs a bit of hand flapping

> It's a winter sport which means it is usually cold so when they bounce everyone watching thinks they are just keeping warm

> They are encouraged to turn around so spinning around looks like they are watching the game from every conceivable angle

> Most of the other children who play are really quite nice because they take their

aggression out on a ball with a stick rather than using their body parts

As a parent when you feel frustrated with the 'system' there is nothing better than picking up a hockey stick and whacking a ball against something

And finally there are no off side rules!

Zac is currently trying out to be the hockey teams goalie. I'll be honest and say we are enjoying whacking balls at him at top speed and it does wonders for sorting out all the sibling rivalry issues. Zac can charge at Walt fully kitted out and Walt can annoy Zac by scoring a few goals past him.

In the most recent, away, league match (Zac's second time in goal, with no formal training) the score was 6-1. We thought there was going to be tears and tantrums but Zac coped well. We saw him banging his leg with frustration a few times when the ball made contact with the back of the goal but we also saw him have a bounce when he managed to save some corking strikes from the opposition. Despite the final score, the team nominated Zac as man of the match. I am not sure if I had ever been prouder and Zac grinned from ear to ear when it was announced.

We do fear for their body parts though

when they play on the field and it can be quite nerve racking when a ball flies across the pitch.  Some parents would worry about their offspring's chances of procreating for us it is more about having a trip to the doctors or the dentist.

Ah, the dentist.  Many parents ask me how we cracked visits to the dentist, it wasn't easy but we are now quite proficient at going especially when it means we are going to have some time off school for an appointment.  The first time we went to the dentist we were allowed to break Zac and Walt in gently.  They would let us wait outside until our appointment slot became available.  This was great in the summer but when it rained it was a bit miserable but then the boys (and I) weren't subjected to the horrid noise of the dentists drill and we didn't have to sit in a confined space with other people who were waiting.  The receptionists would simply come outside and let us know when it was our turn. Having the last appointment of the day also made the experience easier. We worked with the dentist to make small reasonable adjustments.

So then to the dentists chair, this was far trickier and took a lot of appointments, time and patience by the dentist and us.  For starters the chair moves then you have to sit still, then someone puts their hands in your mouth and you are not allowed to bite them,

## Let the Teenage Years Begin

they wear weird tasting gloves and the smells and sounds of the things they use is like nothing else on earth. A complete nightmare for most people, but add a touch of ASD in the mix and it's pure torture. Eventually after a lot of picture schedules, starting out with we say 'hello to Heena" our dentist and "we sit in the chair and it goes up and down". The next visit was the first two steps plus "we open our mouth." The third visit the steps from the first two visits along with "we let Heena put her hands in our mouths." Like toilet training the boys didn't learn that this whole process was okay by watching mum and dad having it done. So we took small steps with big rewards.

On one successful trip the boys were given a special balloon by the dentist as a reward, they were delighted with their red shiny helium filled balloon which read 'healthy teeth and gums" with a picture of a big white smile. Colin and I knew that they were so pleased with the balloons that we could forgo the trip to the McDonalds and just make our way home. We arrived home and as we opened the car door to let the boys out Zac let go of his balloon. He said 'bye bye balloon" and then the tantrum began. It was the tantrum of all tantrums. We tried calming him with all manner of things. We even tried to fob him off with a balloon from McDonalds but he just wasn't having any of it. Eventually he fell asleep from exhaustion and thankfully when he woke up he seemed to have forgotten about the balloon. However, we now know he hadn't forgotten about it because each and every time we visit the dentist they will ask "Would you like a sticker?' or some other gift, Zac will now automatically decline politely with a "No thank you."

In 2009, Walt smashed Zac's face onto the floor, which broke off his adult front teeth. So over the last four years we have had many trips to the dentist for repairs and touch ups. Zac's front teeth have become a bit of a party piece, especially when I forget that he can't bite into solid food. I had forgotten to tell school about the state of his front teeth; after all filled front teeth are usually a long way down the list of things to tell people about when they are working with Zac. The class had been given apples in science, something to do with healthy eating. I received a very panicked call from Zac's Learning Support Assistant to say that they were really sorry but he had bitten into the apple and the whole front section of his teeth just snapped off. The wave of relief could be heard on the other end of the phone when I explained. Of course, Zac thought it was great that he would have to go and have another repair because this ultimately meant another day off school. The school said they would be using bananas next time.

Our current dentist is fantastic, she

*Let the Teenage Years Begin*

adopts a no nonsense approach and is quite abrupt but very kind. She always gives me a quick wink and a wry smile under her mask as she tells the boys, "You will keep the hands down and there will be no moving" and of course they do exactly as she says for fear that she may do something they are not expecting. The boys have grown to really enjoy the bit where the dentist numbers their teeth, scaling and polishing is still not something to be enjoyed but then I can safely say this is the same for me. We recently discovered that our dentist has a son about my age with Asperger's so she totally gets them and again we hope that she will not retire for a very long time. Zac has been for his first visit to the Orthodontist where they mentioned the word 'surgery' before fitting a train track brace; apparently his head will be growing until he is eighteen so maybe we will wait until he is seventeen and half before we query where on the NHS waiting list we are.

Visiting the Doctors had its challenges as well, especially in the early days. One of the surgeries we were registered learnt quickly that it needed to make very small reasonable adjustments to its procedures to help make our visits a little less stressful.

Just after Zac and Walt were diagnosed I noticed that Zac had developed a slight limp and a weakness in his left leg so I decided I would be brave and take both of them to see our GP, just to check it out. When we arrived at the surgery it was quite busy. The waiting area had a very small corner dedicated to entertaining young children, which consisted of a small table and chairs and about five books. This only kept the boys attention for about thirty seconds. There were no iPads or handheld games to amuse them back then (see how wonderful technology is now!) so I managed to keep them still for about a minute. They both decided that they would create their own game of walking in a circle around a quarter of the surgery, giggling as they went past each other. This amused the other patients but not the receptionist. She shouted over the counter "You will need to keep your children under control or we will have to ask you to leave."

So I tried desperately to keep them sat next to me, this made us all get very hot and agitated. The boys started to fuss and cry and then one of the other patients said 'just let them move about, poor things" so I figured that would be fine. The receptionist was really not amused then. She walked from her desk across to where I was sitting and bellowed at me "I have warned you that if you don't keep them under control I will need you to leave."

I should have walked out straightaway but I again tried to keep them in one place. After what seemed like an age we were finally called through. By this time the boys were in a complete state and I was hot and bothered.

The GP we were called through to had obviously had a bad afternoon too. We walked in and he said, "How can I help you?" in a rather gruff bedside manner. So I said, "This is Zac he is having a bit of trouble with his leg." His reply totally shocked me when he barked, "Well I can't examine him in this state!"

As we walked back out to the reception he announced loudly to the waiting patients, "Well if you want to bring him back when he is behaving himself, I can take a better look but I would imagine he will just grow out of it." I was mortified.

We decided to use our favourite skill which has been finely honed over the years and that was to put pen to paper and write the best complaint letter we could. Parents with children who are on the spectrum could pretty much write a great book on how to write letters of complaint and get results. We have to perfect the skill over the years and we live by the phrase "the pen is mightier than the sword" although sometimes you do wonder if the sword would be a quicker option for those who just don't get it!

After a formal meeting with the surgery manager, the lead GP and a representative from the Patient Advice Liaison Service we managed to develop a system where when we telephoned, the receptionist (through gritted teeth) would ask us if we would like a side room where we could wait and she would then take us through to our appointment or the GP could see us in the room we were waiting in which ever was more appropriate on the day. This of course worked fantastically and was a very simple pain free solution for us and it gave the boys a gentler introduction to visiting the surgery. I am sure that the receptionist is still receiving advanced dentistry on her worn out teeth.

Now the boys quite enjoy going along to our GP, although I should point out we are very lucky, as we are now registered with a fantastic health centre which has some really understanding doctors who seem to take the time to understand the boys. The receptionist doesn't mind the games we have to play while we wait. Currently this is a timed 'see how fast I can get all the beads on the bead table from one side to the other'. Like the receptionist I think that the other waiting patients find it most amusing seeing a couple of teenagers and a forty something year old woman competing with each other for the winning time. I am sure if we all thought about it and let our inhibitions go we would actually enjoy playing with some of the toys in a waiting area.

The boys have even started to like to come with me when I have an appointment but only so they can make sure the doctor knows that I have been more grumpy or weird because of my ailment and they absolutely love it when he simply makes a comment like "well it could be your age!"

*Abbey Woolgar*

# School days, the best days of our lives

Are they? For some the answer is YES, mine were certainly. No financial responsibilities, good friends, same routine, great holidays and a source of fun. Certain parts of school life I think did help me define who I am and where I wanted to be.

Now though I constantly tell the boys and myself, that school is a very small part of their life. I was once told that you only spend 6½ hours a day at school and therefore, what happens at home is far more important than school. This is true to some extent but what an impact school can have when things aren't quite going to plan and we just simply don't want to go. No, I am not going to launch into an entire chapter about the education system and Special Educational Needs, it would be too long and ranty right now!

I am constantly trying to be positive, when we are having a 'I don't want to go to school day' or a series of gigantic tantrums we now try to bring the boys attention to the social story™ we have on our kitchen notice board, which reads:

**Getting Ready for School**

*Let the Teenage Years Begin*

I leave for school at 8.00am.

Before I go to school I need to make sure that I am ready for the day.

So that I can concentrate I must have a good breakfast and put all of my breakfast things away when I am finished.

I must put my lunch and drink into my bag and check that I have the right equipment for the day.

People need to smell and look good. I need to clean my teeth, style my hair and use spray and deodorant.

I need to look smart for school so I should check in the mirror to make sure I look okay.

Before we get ready to leave the house we make sure we have left it tidy and that we have turned off all of the lights.

I must make sure I have my coat, bag and

shoes on before 8.00am.

When we walk to school we can say "hello" to people that we know.

While the social story™ gets them out of the front door, anxiety about other students is still our biggest challenge. When we are feeling really annoyed or tired of the constant discussions with school about the same things we ponder the home education system and then reassure ourselves with the theory that the grass is not always greener, and 24/7 with Zac and Walt may be the straw that broke the camels back!

Now I am going to sound very old but some of the kids today really do need a clip round the ear and yes I know that this is politically incorrect! I started to escort them both to Secondary school so that I helped reduce any anxiety and all I can say is I have seen pretty horrible kids and wonder what the youth of today really is coming to. Yep, old person alert.

If I had ever spoken out of turn to an adult in our village when I was growing up my mum would have heard about it and all hell would have let loose. I remember my brother being told off for just hanging out with the wrong people at the wrong time, they hadn't committed a crime but they had all been seen together and one of the girls did something she shouldn't have and every parent was informed of her actions so that they could take action with their own young person. I learnt a lot from my brothers mistakes.

I have continued to escort Zac and Walt part of the way to and from school on my bike with a dog on each side to help me keep up with the boys. I now justify this with two reasons:

1. I get up, get out and get the dogs walked.
2. They need someone to navigate the sea of teenagers.

I have also convinced myself that taking them on my bike is no different to dropping them off at school in the car but I feel I am helping to reduce my carbon footprint and minimising my risk of diabetes.

One afternoon, right across the cycle path was a group of 'teenagers' lighting up, some 50 feet from school. As we approached I rang my bike bell, no reaction as per usual. So, I politely said, "excuse me please can we get through" to which came the reply "go round". Now usually I would have but the road was busy on one side and there is a slight drop on the other. So I stopped and looked the perpetrator in the face. Usually I would try and think of something witty or intelligent to retort with but unfortunately that day my brain just simply gave the response "Just f**k off!" It worked though;

they parted like I was Moses at the Red Sea.  Now each and every time they see me coming they cajole each other and move out of our way.  If I spot one of them outside of school with their parents they always look a bit sheepish.  I did inform the school, just in case the kids had felt intimidated by the mad old woman with the dogs attached to her bike, but the school simply said that "using that type of language was probably the only thing they understood."

On another occasion a young girl, in the same year as the boys decided that she would be clever in front of her friends.  Usually as we passed she would simply call names out at the boys and we would just ignore her immaturity.  I was a bit shocked because I haven't heard the word 'spastic' or 'retard' for many years but that wasn't what was going to shock me the most.

One morning as we made our way to school the girl in question tried to push Walt off his bike.  It was a deliberate push on a bridge, with a twenty odd foot drop down onto four lanes of traffic, travelling on average at 60mph.  Now call me an over protective parent but after witnessing this I have struggled to let the boys walk or cycle to school on their own.

I really struggle with the language that youngsters (yes, old person alert again) use today.  The boys were obviously struggling with it all too. Walt came home saying, "Why do they say 'Innit Blad'". So I responded with "Are you sure that is what they are saying?" Walt was adamant that 'yes' this is what was being said. So I had to be honest and say "I have no idea what that means". A few days later I asked one of the other kids what "Blad" meant. He said he didn't know. So I asked how it was spelt. He said "B-L-A-D" to which I responded, "Would that not be short for bladder?" The boys found this highly amusing and I think they have a little chuckle to themselves every time they now hear someone saying it.

The urban dictionary defines it as 'blad' being the London pronunciation of the word. It actually comes from Jamaica and comes from the meaning of brother, of part of ones blood line, saying that someone is close to them. We live about fifty five miles from London and about four thousand six hundred and sixty miles from Jamaica so I am still not entirely sure why it is necessary to use it at school. There are so many abbreviations and strange phrases used now that the urban dictionary has now become a friend like Google just so I can keep up with any questions the boys may have.

The boys are pretty good now at understanding that some words can have two meanings and should only be used in the right context. On one of our holidays to America the boys were enjoying going on the same waterslide over and over again. They had been told repeatedly to 'sit on their butts' by one of the lifeguards but when the lifeguards changed over, they were suddenly told not to sit on their butts but to, 'sit on their fannies'. Now you and I know that in America this means bottom but for the boys this was very confusing especially when you have just started secondary school!

I should point out that homework and autism simply do not mix and of course at secondary school there is a lot of it.

Why would you want to bring work home from school to do? There is simply no logic to it. School is school and home is home, so why should the two ever go together. It would be like mixing poo with a delicious dessert and saying it was "very tasty."

When we found out that the boy's school offered a homework club every day immediately after school, we were delighted. We were even more delighted when the boys said how much fun it was. The relief of not having to remember how to solve a quadratic equation and the rhetoric contained in the complete works of Shakespeare was immense; that is, until the homework club had a week off.

On the walk home, we chatted amongst ourselves about the prospect of all of us sitting down together to deal with the sheer horror of the dreaded homework. So the foundations were laid. We positioned ourselves strategically at the kitchen table – the same one that I used to do my own homework when I was the same age as the boys. I placed myself between them so that I could help both at the same time; they were far enough apart not to disrupt each other. Soon we were off.

Zac had two pieces of homework, history and R.E. He started on the history homework, which required him to draw a medieval picture of how religion may well have been viewed in those days. I was waiting for him to ask me what it was like in the medieval times but thankfully I think he thinks I was only around for the World Wars. The picture Zac drew looked great; it looked very much like a Monty Python sketch. There was a giant foot in the centre, a couple of strange-looking devils in hell, a few odd-looking angels and finally some random pictures of what Zac described as "things of pleasure and pain."

I suggested that once Zac had finished his picture he should move onto the R.E homework. In this he was asked to write about Jesus and who he was. Meanwhile, I began to help colour in his artwork while at the same time helping Walt with his homework. I assured Zac that if he needed help, then I would help him to think about what sentences he could write.

Walt's homework, technology, took the form of a word search. Now in my day - and I'm sounding rather old here again – but homework did not consist of a word search. As a youngster, I used to get excited about going on holiday because I could have the latest bumper book of word searches to do on the journey. So over the years, how is it that word searches have turned from pleasure to pain, and when did they become an educational tool?

After a long hour spent colouring and trying to find what seemed to be an everlasting list of male-orientated words in a tiny print word search (I still have no idea what anthropometrics and a ball pein hammer are) I turned to Zac. He had written four words for his R.E. homework: "Jesus is a man". So I said to him: "Well that's stating the obvious, Zac. Think about what Jesus did."

After a few short moments and some more colouring in between word search squinting, Zac piped up 'How do you spell obvious?" I asked him "What have you written, Zac?" He replied innocently "Jesus is a man that's stating the ..."

We have had a number of other homework hilarities, including a maths problem, which said:

*A missile contains three sections; head, body and tail. The head of a missile is 12 inches long. The tail is as long as the head plus half the body. The body is as long as the head and the tail together. How long is the missile altogether?*

Zac's answer after about two hours of trying various mathematical equations and phoning a friend was "Let's just put that it exploded!"

Walt brought home a food technology crossword, again when did crosswords become homework I asked. After a lot of internet searching and a Skype call to the grandparents we gave up trying to find the real answers to the following questions:

*Liquid or other substance.* (It began with the letter b then there were five spaces and it ended with an r.)

We put beeeeer.

*What should be kept at below minus 15 degrees* (seven letters second letter e.)

We put penguin!

After a few more word search homework tasks Zac announced that he wants to be a word search vegan.

In Science, I am so grateful that we have not had any sex education homework but it has proved to be an interesting field of discussion. The boys came home from school and said "Mum we are doing s-e-x at school but we are not doing any practical's." I could only reply "thank heavens for that!" Walt mentioned the other day as we went past the clothing shop, 'Superdry', "they sell condoms in there you know," after a little chuckle, I corrected him and took him along to 'Superdrug' to show him the difference. As we walked away from Superdrug Walt said, "Mum, what is bum sex?" Not 100% sure but I would guess this was not covered as part of the national curriculum.

What still amazes me is how sometimes the boys won't tell you what happened at school when it actually happened but it will come out months, sometimes years later. A month or so ago Zac announced, "In Year 2, I got my willy out in the playground, Mrs. Lee says "put it away Zac," I was in a lot of trouble." Walt said matter of factly about a year ago, "when I first started my new school I didn't understand which changing rooms I should go in for P.E. so I went into the girls changing room, they screamed a lot." I dread to think what else will come from Secondary school in the years to come!

There are times though when what is said or done at school has a huge impact on the boys immediately. This was the case when recently Zac started to develop an obsession with hygiene and bacteria. At first we made light of it, you have to when you have a messy Walt and two very bacteria infested hounds living in the house but once the obsession became almost an OCD trait we needed to find out what had happened to spark this strange new behaviour. Apparently, in Science the class had been asked to wipe a hand onto an agar jelly plate and then record how much it had grown over a short period of time. This of course (because it is very visual) had completely freaked Zac out to the point that he started to wash his hands very frequently even before, during and after mealtimes.

Over the summer I persuaded Zac and Walt to try eating in the main canteen at school, so that they did not have to watch and criticise each others eating habits. Zac apparently eats too loudly and Walt is just very messy and unhygienic. But the school seemed to have developed a different approach to this and have set up what Zac calls the 'Special table'. Unfortunately they had both been watching an episode of Family Guy called "Petarded" just before this was implemented and so this has not gone down well with them at all.

In the episode Peter Griffin (the dad character) is given a low IQ score and is therefore, dubbed as being mentally retarded or special. There is a scene where Peter introduces his state appointed inspirational social worker named Verne, which is a reference to the 1988 movie Rain Man in which the character Verne is Raymond Babbitt's "main man".

The boys haven't seen Rain Man but they know about it and that is some how connected to autism. So now when the boys refer to the 'special table' at school they will go "high five", clap their hands repeatedly and laugh uncontrollably. Let's just hope they don't ever feel the need to perform another line from the episode and go into a fast food restaurant (or the school canteen, heaven forbid) and shout into the microphone "Attention all restaurant customers. Testicles. That is all."

*Let the Teenage Years Begin*

# Sex, Lies, Videotape and a hint of music thrown in for good measure

Now some of you may be thinking, "Why are they letting those boys watch Family Guy? It is totally inappropriate for their age!" Well if you are one of those people, this chapter may well not be for you. Please feel free to skip to the next one.

Our primary reason for allowing them the opportunity to view it was that some of the jokes went straight over their heads. This has recently changed as you will see in later in this chapter but it also allowed them to understand some of the conversations that the other children were having at school. We of course watch it with them and we can then monitor how much of it is appropriate and delete the episodes that are totally inappropriate. Zac and Walt tend, like most children on the spectrum, to watch the same thing over and over again until they can repeat large chunks of it. They really enjoy the episodes, which contain film parodies like Star Wars, Taken, The Wizard of Oz and a whole host of Disney film references and so you kind of justify that it can't all be that bad and it will aid their sense of humour.

One film we almost regretted the boys

watching over and over again was the 'Kings Speech' I should point out that this was only because of the timing. Walt had been taking part in a Community Champions project at school and had really thrown himself into it. It was all about following rules on how to behave in the community, right up his street. I received a telephone call from his class teacher to say he had been selected to go to the local Radio station the next day to tell them how he had become a Community Champion. Of course I said, "yes" without a thought.

We got up early and made our way to the office where the live show was taking place and were ushered into the studio. As we stood waiting for our slot, I spotted a microphone similar to the one in the film and the full horror of what might happen hit me. At the end of the film Lionel Logue conducts King George VI's speech to the nation with a series of mouthed swear words to help him overcome his stammer. Walt stood in front of the mic and started to mouth words and as he limbered up I could clearly see him mouthing, "Bloody bugger to you, you beastly bastard." Timed, just like Geoffrey Rush in the film.

Thankfully the microphone wasn't switched on. When he was finally interviewed he was superb. He told everyone about a movie he had seen (not the Kings Speech, thank goodness!) but one about a naughty boy as he put it and then he went on to tell everyone listening, "one my lines is well, basically, if you are playing out in the park and its really new and painted and someone tells you to scratch it then you should say "no", go home and go and tell your parents."  The DJ chortled at his concise instructional delivery and then simply said "Walter has had his say, thank you." The warm up must have helped him to get into character, just like George VI.  I was just relieved that he hadn't said, "Fuck. Fuck! Fuck, fuck, fuck and fuck! Fuck, fuck and bugger! Bugger, bugger, buggerty buggerty buggerty, fuck, fuck, arse!" like Colin Firth.

It is a difficult time when you realise that your children understand the things that you swear you didn't know until you were much older.  We realised that Zac and Walt both knew what 'fuck" actually meant when they were about 10 but they had said it out loud, out of context of course, for the first time when they were just four years old.  In my memory this word didn't exist until I was at least 14 and then I blamed Arnold Schwarzenegger introducing me to it.

Imagine my horror then when Zac, Walt and I were watching a programme, which contained a man sitting behind a desk and then the camera panned round to a woman on her hands and knees under the desk.  In the context of the clip it was a funny moment so I allowed myself a little snigger. Walt immediately asked me "mum, why are you laughing?" Now if my quick-witted husband had been about he would have replied with something like "how lazy of the man that he can't pick up his own pencil!" No, I said, "because it's funny" so Walt said "what that she is giving him a blow job?"

Shocked would describe my reaction to his comment. So I thought, 'I'll test the waters out here and see if he actually knows what that is?' Mistake. Of course he knew. I said "Walt, do you know what a blow job is?" He said "Yes, that is where a lady sucks a man's penis." Sex education at school had paid off then as he was using the correct anatomical description.

Of course I decided that at that point it was past our bedtime and we should all turn in for the night. When Colin returned from work I told him what Walt had admitted to knowing. "That's my boy" wasn't his reaction but like me there was a little snigger. So the next morning we said "Walt do you remember what a blow job is?" He said "Oh yes, that is where a lady does naked dancing and men give her money." We had to correct him and say "No Walt that is a form of prostitution." Of course he then corrected himself and graphically described the act again. All I can hope is that these two things don't get confused again in his head.

While puberty has bought its challenges we are not quite in the realms of some of the other parents who have children on the spectrum. I remember hearing a story about a boy who would masturbate every time the theme tune for the six o'clock news came on. This was okay as long as his grandparents weren't visiting at six o'clock.

However, one of the saddest but probably the most amusing stories I heard was about a young lad who desperately wanted a pet. He had asked his mum and she had said, "no it would be far too much work". So having learnt in sex education at school, that sperm were like tadpoles he decided that he would grow his own pet frog under his bed. His mum discovered a large bowl under his bed when she was cleaning and when she questioned him on it he proudly told his mum that growing in the bowl were his own tadpoles to make his own pet frog. Now whether this is an urban myth or not I will certainly be keeping my eye open for any bowls under the boys bed and monitoring their viewing of the six o'clock news. For now though the boys have just been afraid of "catching puberty".

One of the films, which kind of helped me understand parts of life, were some of the Monty Pythons films my favourite though was the 'Life of Brian'. My mum had the audio version of the film in the early 1980's and we used to listen to it over and over again on long car journeys. I am sure I didn't understand half of the jokes but I know having watched some of the films again with the boys that they do understand a lot more than I did at their age. And surely watching the Life of Brian is now good for the Religious Education lessons at school isn't it? It kind of tells the story of Jesus and someone once said to me that the bible is probably one of the best social stories™ of all time so can I argue that the Life of Brian is a social story™ too? And no one can argue that the song lyrics in "Always look on the bright side of life" are not good for the soul.

My taste in music is an interesting blend; some would say it is eclectic and some would describe it as downright terrible. The boys would describe it is as the latter, especially if I dare sing along to it.

It is obviously a parent's prerogative to embarrass his or her children with their tastes in music, but I take it one step further.

In the early 1980's my brother introduced us to Chris de Burgh. Some would say he is like Marmite, you either love it or hate it. I love him so much so I think I am on the 20th concert this year. Colin has been dragged to about 17 of these and I have already dragged the boys along to two of them and I am sure there will be more to follow. Last year Walt, my mum and I sat downstairs at Birmingham Symphony Hall while Zac and

*Let the Teenage Years Begin*

Colin preferred to sit up in the gods.

During some of the shows Chris de Burgh emerges from the side door and walks through the audience (usually singing Lady in Red) and does a kind of meet and greet the audience bit. I have been lucky enough on a couple of occasions to have been sung to and have had my hand kissed and a quick hug. This may make some people feel a bit queasy so again you have the option to skip to the next chapter here if you choose to. So this time was no different except that Walt was there. Chris de Burgh approached and sung a few lines as he walked towards us. My mum grabbed him and gave him a hug and then he approached me kissed my hand, sang a line and moved to Walt.

Walt had a little bounce of excitement and then shook Chris de Burgh's hand. Chris de Burgh returned to the stage and as the song stopped Walt was clearly heard by our section of the audience shouting, "Is that the real Chris de Burgh?" At least ten ladies in red dresses assured him that it was.

As we prepared for the most recent concert, Zac announced, "Chris de Burgh is an underrated artist" to which Walt responded, "Don't say that out loud". We are still not sure whether Walt said this as a street cred thing or whether it was fear that ten or so ladies dressed in red would lynch his brother! What we did make sure was that we could not sit anywhere near the targeted areas for the Lady in Red wooing just in case Walt grabbed the mic and shouted "Are you really the real Chris de Burgh!"

You will be pleased to read that we haven't just exposed them to Chris de Burgh.  We took them to see Peter Gabriel and recently we went to see Passenger.  We thought they would enjoy Passenger purely because he swears a little bit in some of his songs and that is "a bit naughty!"  After the concert we asked them, "How was the concert?"  Zac had to point out that we had been to "a gig" not a concert and that if we were to go again he would like to sit not stand and we should make sure that there were no horrid drunk ladies!  So we are not 100% sure if he actually enjoyed the music side of it.  I had started to worry about my influence on their music tastes but I can safely say Zac has now started to listen to his own music genre in the form of a group called 'Dragonforce'.  The only way I can describe their music is that it is like listening to something from a 1980's cartoon, like Thundercats.  Zac listens to the same three tracks over and over again but we have invested in headphones so that he can enjoy it without any comments from those who apparently don't appreciate a good bit of music!

I was introduced to REM during my first year of university.  Now I am not sure whether it was just me but sometimes I found it difficult to make out the actual lyrics in the songs. For years, I would drive from Bournemouth to home or to see Colin at Coventry University singing at the top of my voice "That's me in my car" to the chorus of the song 'Texarkana' which of course I know now, having had many people point it out to me, that it is clearly "Catch me if I fall". So how delighted I was when we realised that the boys had inherited my wondrous lyric ability.

The first time we noticed it we just thought, "bless them." But as they have got older we have thought "thank goodness for that".

As all current teenagers the boys like to listen to what is trending on YouTube or on Spotify but they also like to listen to music, which is a bit different. When they asked if I could down load some LMFAO I agreed. The first couple of tracks were great, I managed to get the non-explicit versions but one of the songs "Shots" was not available as a non-explicit version. Yes, I should have known but I figured if it had any naughty words I could safely know that the boys would know what they were and that they also knew that they weren't allowed to say them. So I listened to the track first before allowing the boys carte blanche. I listened to it with horror and swore that I would not allow the boys to listen to such things until they were much much older.

Now the problem with iTunes is the iCloud!  I had plugged my iPhone into Colin's car, via Bluetooth (it all gets far too technical for me at this point) and off we went not realizing that the Shots song had synced to my phone.  As I was chatting to Colin, I didn't realise which song had started to play but yep 'Shots' was mid track by the point of realisation.  The next thing I know Walt is in hysterics in the back of the car, so I asked him, "What's so funny matey?" knowing full well that he would probably repeat the actual lyrics seeing as he had been asked but to my amusement and relief he said, "It's disgusting.  Why would ladies want to suck guts?"  Now if you don't know the lyrics to this song, I would suggest that you Google them.

Zac requested a drum kit for his birthday so we thought that an Xbox Guitar Hero drum kit would be a good place to start.  As the game began both boys decided to have a go, Zac on the drums and Walt on the microphone.  The noise was an interesting cacophony so Colin and I stayed downstairs. When they came down to lunch, Zac said "Come on Walt eat up we need to go and learn some more Banana Raspberry."  So I said, "which song is that then?" "You know", said Zac "the one the Muppets did, I'm just a poor boy from a poor family scabby moose, scabby moose can you do the fandango one."

*Let the Teenage Years Begin*

Of course he meant Bohemian Rhapsody by Queen but now for us it will always be referred to as the Banana Raspberry or Scabby Moose song.

*Abbey Woolgar*

# It's really just the beginning

People often think or say "Should you have written about Zac and Walt like this?" and my reply comes two fold. Firstly; it is great to write all the things down that we have done and experienced and look back on them and say, "Gosh that was tough and then reflect and say well we have come along way." The second is; Zac and Walt will one day read all of these, should I worry about the content. No, they will quite possibly never apply the content to themselves and besides I don't think any of the stories contained in the books would embarrass or shock them. In fact, Walt has read snippets and he finds them "funny". This year on his Christmas list, he has put this book and 'Just Another Mum'. That's my boy! But let's hope Santa thinks he has been a good boy!

Everyday I remind myself of all the changes and challenges the boys have been through. The biggest parenting change has been that they are now less physically challenging (except for the expectation that I will be their personal hockey coach) but they are now far more mentally challenging.

Physically, like all teenagers, the boys have changed. Walt marked the 17th October as the day he grew taller than his mum and I reminded him that day; that just because he was taller than me, it didn't mean I couldn't still tell him off! Like most parents I find telling them off looking upwards instead of downwards a strange concept but the joy of Autism is that I don't get the back chat from them, well at least not out loud!

Colin and I commented the other day when Walt walked into the kitchen for breakfast that it now seemed we had two more men living in the house with us. Of course Walt actually thought we had two more men in the house and he piped up and said "Well they are not living in my room."

We are living in a house now that could easily be converted for the boys to give them a couple of self contained housing units. We could convert the garage and it's vast loft space for one of the boys and the top floor of the house is already pretty much a home on it's own, it has a shower room, and two good living areas with the potential to convert the landing area into a small kitchen. We are still aiming as part of their transition to adulthood that they live away from us, if possible. Most young people struggle to get a deposit for their own place now so having the boys at home (living semi-independently) would not be something that would be out of the ordinary.

I am still keeping my fingers crossed that a nice girl will come and sweep them off their feet. Walt says he has two girl friends to consider at the moment. He doesn't still get that you actually have to ask someone to be in a relationship with you but at least we are on the right lines. He looked indignant when I pointed out that he might actually have to inform the two girls he was considering. Zac continues to develop his sense of humour when it comes to the ladies and he likes nothing more than winding his brother up about potential girlfriends. We often catch him practicing his cheesy one-liners. This afternoon he leant on the bonnet of Colin's company car (a very corporate grey Ford Mondeo) and said "hello ladies". We had to point out that a Grey Ford Mondeo really wasn't a babe magnet and that God would need to help any poor girl who fell for that kind of chat up line!

Mentally the boys are quite exhausting. There is a constant need to repeat simple instructions. Trying to keep up with a conversation with them is so often like trying to put a moving jigsaw puzzle together. The constant questions about facts and figures is draining and woe betide you if you make an answer up on the spur of the moment. We have learnt that we will be asked the same question again sometime later and if we haven't remembered exactly what we said there will be further interrogation.

The most tiring of all is listening to them recite an entire episode of a programme they have watched. This is usually at the end of a day when you just need to sit and listen to your own thoughts for five minutes, this is lovingly known as the 'chunter time'. I have developed the phrase 'really', nodding head and looking interesting gaze but they aren't fools, they will always say "Are you listening to me?" in exactly the same way I intonate that very same phrase to them when I am ask them to put their shoes on.

It still seems that the simple 'common sense' things floor them. If you ask them to try on some new trousers they will strip off (to their birthday suit) and then put their pants and socks back on to try on the new trousers. Walt has recently started to ask a question every time you give him a task to do. So if I say, "Walt can you please go and run the bath?" He will say, "How do I do that?" We know he knows how to run the bath but we are still working out if he just needs a bit or reassurance that he will do it right or whether he just feels he should talk! These are the things that frustrate me but I should simply see them as their idiosyncrasies'. Maybe I will start to love these quirks in time.

Having an insight into the transition process for young people with Special Educational Needs opened my eyes to what we needed to do in order to give the boys the best possible life chances. There are a whole host of professional people who get involved in the formal process that it can sometimes be a minefield and sometimes there is the expectation that someone else could do it all for us.

There is so much that can be done to help young people on the autistic spectrum but it needs to be done at an early age. Yes, it is tough sometimes but perseverance; taking responsibility for your child and knowing that sometimes the little things will make all the difference really do help.

Zac and Walt might well live in the house of mum and dad when they are older but we are getting them used to doing simple domestic chores with the view that one day they will be able to do it them themselves without support.

Managing bills and money still needs some work but there is still time for this and I am pretty sure that money management is a skill that I am still learning. I am pretty sure Colin would tell you that he is still supporting me in this area.

Preparing meals is slowly developing. The

boys are now able to make their own packed lunches, occasionally they need prompting but probably just like any other teenager. They are starting to understand recipes and they enjoy planning and cooking the Saturday family meal. We hope that every day won't be a lasagne day but at least they will know how to feed themselves.

I met a parent who said that she wouldn't let her son anywhere near a toaster because he didn't understand the concept of heat and therefore, she felt that he would never be able to cook for himself. After a quick chat with her she said that his favourite food when he got home from school was Pop Tarts. So I suggested that she stuck a contact thermometer to the toaster this would then change colour as the toaster heated up. When the toaster was hot the thermometer would show a red indicator and when it started to cool it would go orange and it would be safe to remove the Pop Tart when the thermometer went green. This would hopefully help him understand when something cooked was safe to touch. Then later on she could introduce oven gloves and using utensils for more complicated cooking. Sometimes, lateral thinking and common sense approaches can go out of the window when you are a parent to a child with ASD. The reason for this is that we are usually exhausted! We always need to remember that no one and nothing is perfect but most of all we need to just peek out of the box and remember that some basic but creative ideas will often be the solution to some of the problems right in front of us. This is often "easier said than done" when the problems seem out of your control.

Getting Zac and Walt work worries me. Having worked on Adult training and Youth training programmes in my early twenties for about six years, I witnessed how hard it was for people who were in any way slightly different.

One of the adult trainees I worked with, a man in his early forties (who now I would know straightaway was on the spectrum) needed a lot of support not with the IT based work he was completing but with his relationships with his colleagues. The actual work he did was outstanding and his placement always recognized this but what let him down was his social understanding. I attended numerous placement reviews where he was told not to sit so close to colleagues, to take care of his personal hygiene and to stop making comments out loud especially when customers were present. These are the sorts of things I worry about with Zac and Walt. They may well achieve GCSE's at grades 'C' and above but will they have the social skills to sell themselves at an interview and then sustain working relationships? I do know that my current mission is to get them as job ready as I possibly can.

I am finding it hard enough to secure work for myself, hence the book writing, so I dread to think how challenging this will be for Zac and Walt. They have both joked with me about writing their own book but it would be about me. I dread to think what it might entail but I know it will include their unique comedy prose. Who knows maybe they could develop a stand up routine to go alongside it?

Our ultimate employment dream would be to set up a business that Zac and Walt can help run if all else fails. Colin has considered doing a plumbing course so that we could create 'Woolgar & Sons' and I have a dream of opening a bed and breakfast in the wilds of Scotland or North Wales. Walt says that if we do set up a bed and breakfast he would take people on fishing trips. We have suggested that he might like to try fishing first and that there will always be lots of other jobs that he could do but when we mentioned the word 'cleaning' he seemed to change the subject. Funny that!

Zac has his heart set on climbing as many mountains as he can so we suggested that if we found the right location he could do 'Zac's Mountain tours' from the bed and breakfast for the guests.  At the moment, I am not sure that people would be able to keep up with him as he has an ability to scale a hill without getting out of breath and he doesn't really care if he leaves the rest of his party behind.  This would need a lot of work before he became a millionaire from it!

In the last 12 months we have climbed Snowdon, Ben Nevis and Kinder Scout.  I am not sure that I am up to the 3 Peaks Challenge but Zac says he is.  Once we have walked up Scafell Pike I think, I might try and convince him that we have done the 3 Peaks and hope that he doesn't realise what the challenge bit is.  Whenever he walks up a mountain he comes alive and it is something that we think he will pursue into adulthood.  When we walked up Ben Nevis, he bought a tear to my eye, not just because he was walking so quickly and the pain was starting to show, but because we went through a cloud and on the other side he said "Mum, I think we might be in heaven, do you think we might see Granddad Roger up here?" Their view of the world is sometimes so much better than my own.

Zac keeps announcing that he is on spectrum but that he isn't mentally disabled but just that he sees things differently.  We bought him a book called 'Different Like Me" it seemed age appropriate and not too dreary and we thought it might help him understand a little more about ASD. Zac took one look at it and said, "You know what, we are all different, I am not going to be Bill Gates or Albert Einstein, I will be me." Another proud mum moment finally after the years of telling them that they are Walt and Zac, and not a label, have paid off.

## About the Author

Over the last 10 years, Abbey has presented her story to many parents and professionals. She hopes that this book and her first book 'Just Another Mum' will help others enjoy Autism.

Abbey is a qualified Trainer and NVQ Assessor/Verifier. She has 20 years' work experience across a variety of private and public sector organisations.

Abbey now runs her own company, Flirdigan Training and Consultancy. But still her most important work role, to date is that of looking after her two children, two dogs and a husband.